Coral Reefs

BY

Sylvia A. Earle

ILLUSTRATED BY

Bonnie Matthews

NATIONAL GEOGRAPHIC

WASHINGTON, D.C.

To Russell, Kevin, Taylor, Morgan, and other children of the 21st century.
May the coral reefs in their future be as healthy and beautiful as those I knew as a child.
~SAE

For my brother, Larry, whose adventurous spirit has always inspired me;
and to Anne with love and thanks for her support.
~BM

How would you like to visit the underwater world of the coral reef?

Snorkel

In warm, clear oceans around the world, coral reefs circle our Earth like a belt of beautiful jewels.

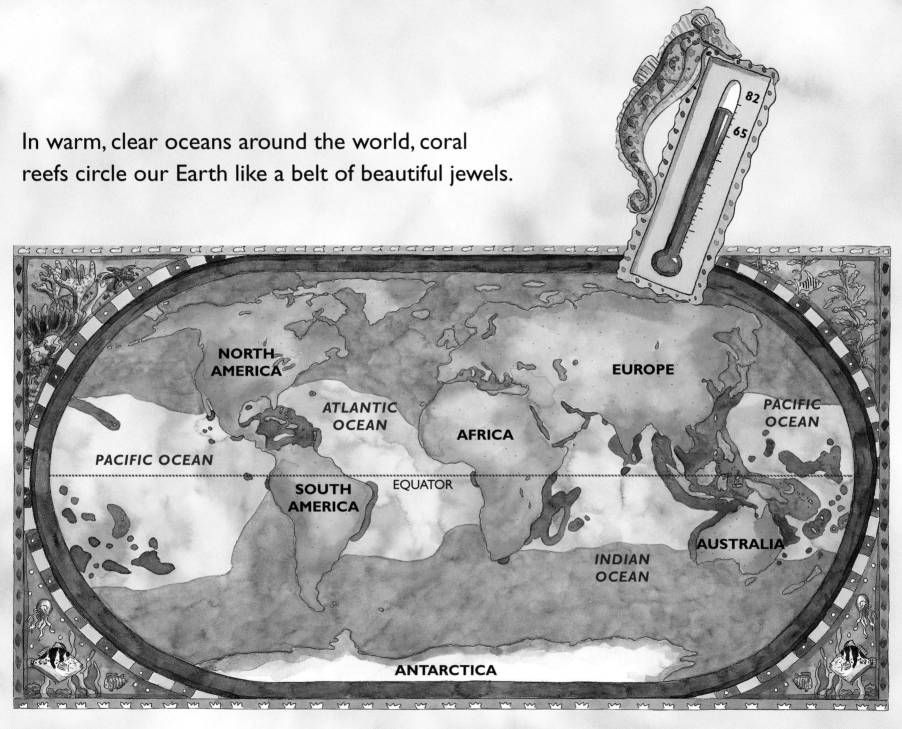

82
65

NORTH AMERICA

EUROPE

ATLANTIC OCEAN

PACIFIC OCEAN

AFRICA

PACIFIC OCEAN

EQUATOR

SOUTH AMERICA

AUSTRALIA

INDIAN OCEAN

ANTARCTICA

■ Coral reef   ■ Coral reef water temperature zone

Coral reefs are like rainbow-colored cities. Even the "buildings" are alive. Day and night, many creatures are out swimming around. Others peek from cracks and holes.

Humans can't breathe underwater like a fish can, but you can still visit coral reefs. Strap on a face mask, snorkel, and flippers and come along!

Corals belong to a group of animals that have soft, jelly-like bodies. They all have slippery arms with tiny stinging cells. Jellyfish, anemones, and sea fans are among their many relatives.

Coral

Sea fan

Anemone

Jellyfish

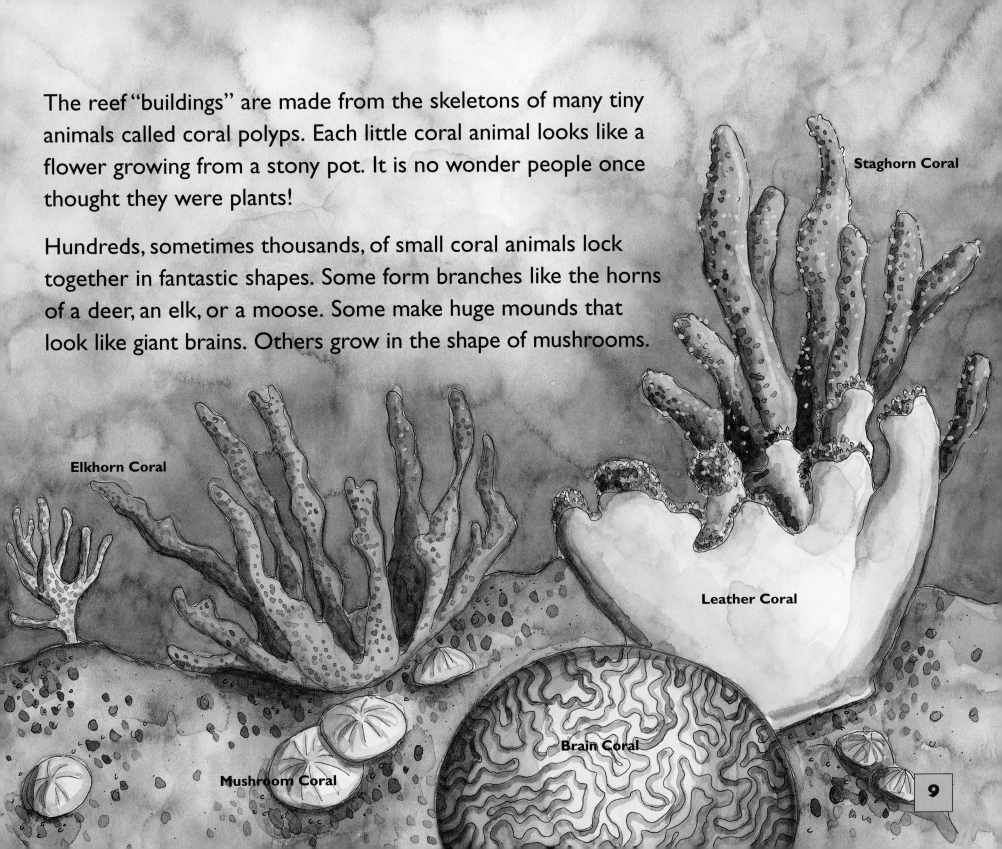

The reef "buildings" are made from the skeletons of many tiny animals called coral polyps. Each little coral animal looks like a flower growing from a stony pot. It is no wonder people once thought they were plants!

Hundreds, sometimes thousands, of small coral animals lock together in fantastic shapes. Some form branches like the horns of a deer, an elk, or a moose. Some make huge mounds that look like giant brains. Others grow in the shape of mushrooms.

Staghorn Coral

Elkhorn Coral

Leather Coral

Brain Coral

Mushroom Coral

9

Coral reefs grow in shallow, clear, warm water.
Once a year, a few days after the last full moon of summer,
reef corals release their eggs into the sea.
The eggs grow into little larvae—baby corals—that drift for several weeks.

Close-up view of larvae

Young corals need a rocky bottom or other hard surface to grow on. Sometimes they settle on shipwrecks. They can grow into beautiful shapes that make the wrecks look like coral castles.

For reef-building corals to grow, the temperature has to be just right—not too hot, not too cold. There must also be just the right amount of salt in the water—not too much, not too little. And reef corals need sunlight to grow.

Hundreds of tiny plants shaped like jellybeans live inside each soft coral animal. They make the corals colorful—green, blue, gold, pink, or sometimes even pale purple.

Fan coral

Brain coral

Coral close-ups

When everything is just right, reef-building corals build hard skeletons around their soft bodies. The corals divide many times, and lock together to form reefs. These are the buildings in the underwater city.

Elkhorn coral

Sea squirts

So who lives in this underwater city? Millions of creatures! Some are short, round, and hollow. Others are long and slim. A few look like stars or pincushions. Many are very small.

Sponge

Anemone

Sea urchin

Snail

Scallops

Clams

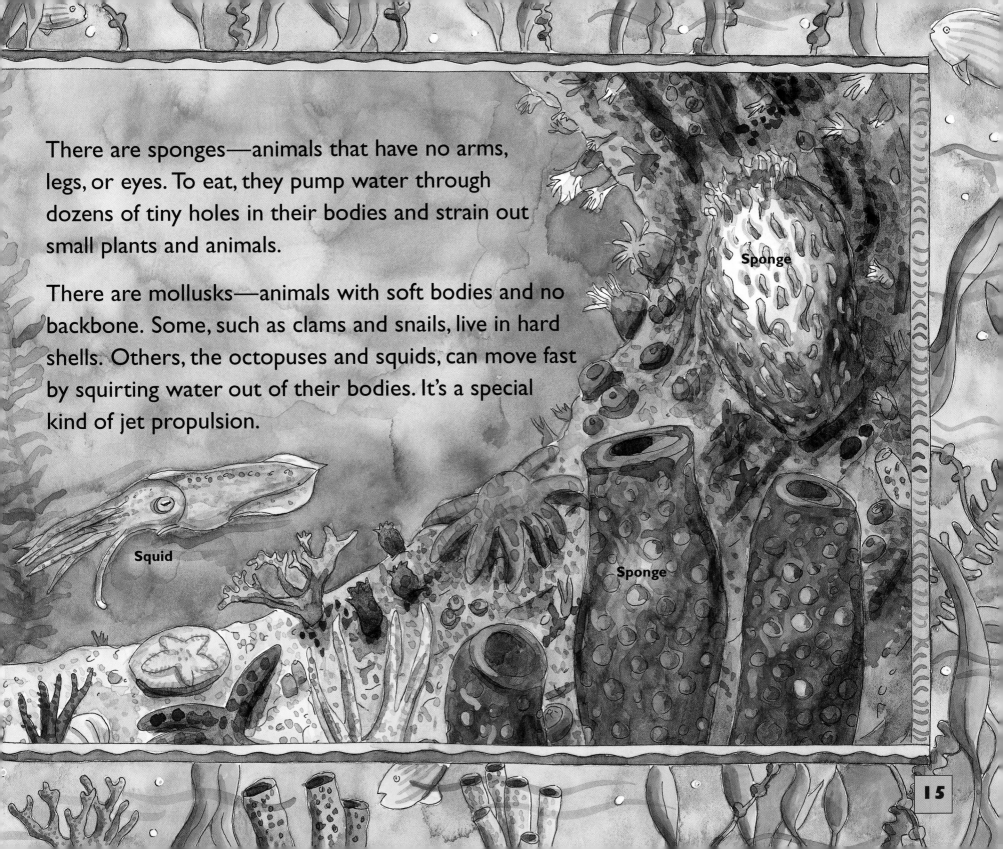

There are sponges—animals that have no arms, legs, or eyes. To eat, they pump water through dozens of tiny holes in their bodies and strain out small plants and animals.

There are mollusks—animals with soft bodies and no backbone. Some, such as clams and snails, live in hard shells. Others, the octopuses and squids, can move fast by squirting water out of their bodies. It's a special kind of jet propulsion.

Sponge

Squid

Sponge

There are also sea stars, sea cucumbers, serpent stars, and sand dollars—the spiny-skinned animals. They move using their hundreds of feet with suckers on the end.

Some reef animals are soft on the inside but have their "skeleton" on the outside. Look at the crabs, lobsters, and shrimp! Each leg, each long antenna, even each eye is covered in a stiff outer shell. As they grow, they split out of their old shells. Then new shells form. It's like they're changing into larger clothes.

Serpent star

Hermit crab

Sea cucumber

Sea star

Sand dollars

Spiny lobster

Shrimp

Sea star

Sea star

Christmas tree worm

Many types of worms live on the reef, too,
but they're not like the earthworms you know.
Some are bright and fancy, such as
Christmas tree worms. Others are very small
and hide deep within the corals.

And of course, there are fish. All fish have a backbone, beautiful eyes, a heart, and a brain. About one quarter of all of the kinds of fish known in the sea live around coral reefs.

Butterfly fish

Angelfish

Clown triggerfish

Grouper

There are parrotfish, as bright as tropical birds, with a mouth that looks a lot like a parrot's beak. Bright yellow, silver, and black butterfly fish dance about, usually in pairs, sometimes in groups called schools. There are angelfish, as gentle as kittens, grouper, as playful as puppies, damselfish, that move like dancers, and hundreds of others.

Damselfish

Parrotfish

Many reef dwellers find food in nearby meadows of seagrasses. Some eat tiny creatures that float over the reef.

Mangroves

Seagrasses

Pufferfish

Snapper

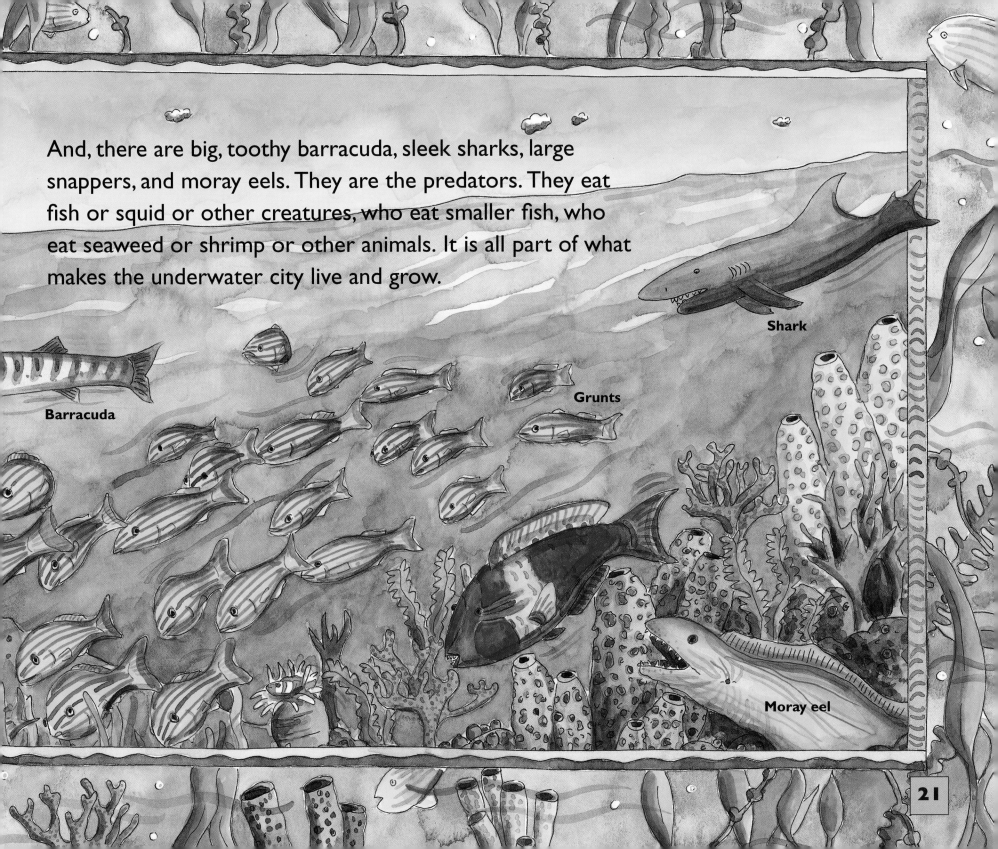

And, there are big, toothy barracuda, sleek sharks, large snappers, and moray eels. They are the predators. They eat fish or squid or other creatures, who eat smaller fish, who eat seaweed or shrimp or other animals. It is all part of what makes the underwater city live and grow.

Shark

Barracuda

Grunts

Moray eel

Just as cities have tourists, reefs have special visitors.
Sometimes, sea turtles glide by, or pause for an underwater
nap. Hawksbill turtles come to munch on their favorite reef
sponges. Green sea turtles come to snack on seagrasses.
Big loggerhead turtles may stop to search for a jellyfish lunch.
Like turtles, dolphins may visit and then slip away to the
open sea.

Hawksbill turtle

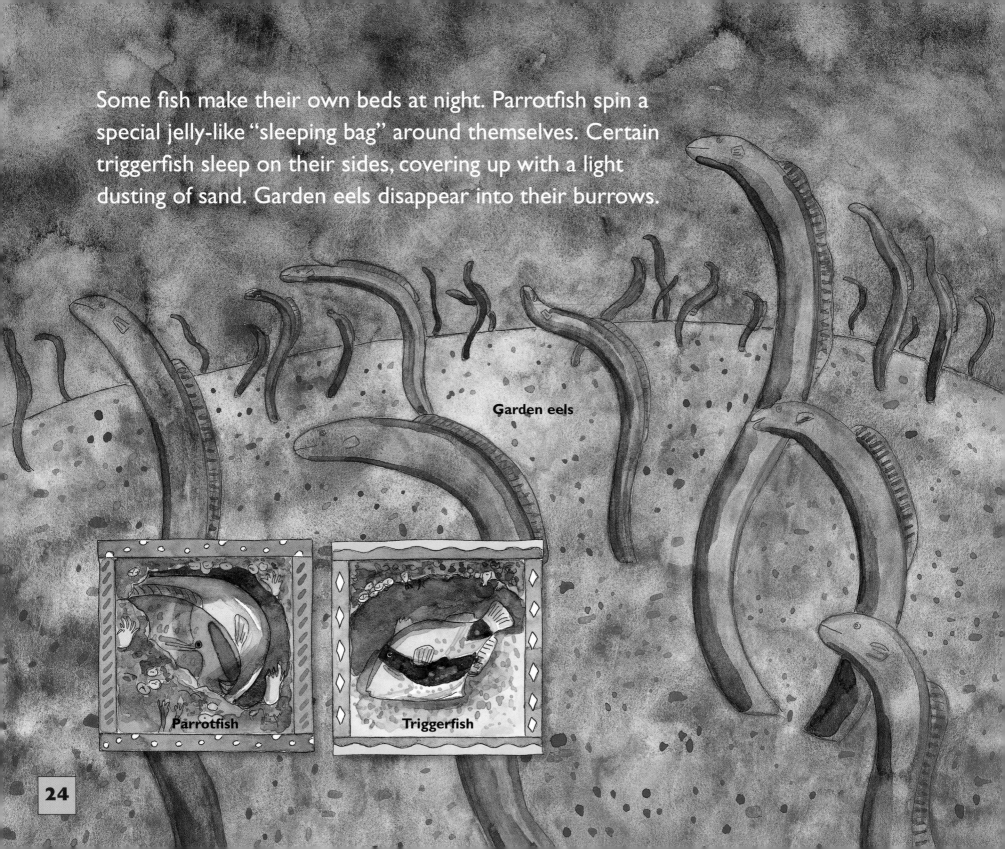

Some fish make their own beds at night. Parrotfish spin a special jelly-like "sleeping bag" around themselves. Certain triggerfish sleep on their sides, covering up with a light dusting of sand. Garden eels disappear into their burrows.

Garden eels

Parrotfish

Triggerfish

But coral reefs, like other great cities, never sleep. At night, many creatures come out of hiding places. Bright red squirrel fish swim out of small caves. Basket starfish, curled up by day, spread their arms wide at night to feed.

Swimming over a reef at night, you may find yourself covered with sparkling lights. Thousands of small, swimming creatures light up the sea. Tiny shrimp produce brilliant puffs of light. Jellyfish glow.

Jellyfish

Shrimp

Basket starfish

Squirrel fish

Some coral reefs are much larger than our biggest cities. The Great Barrier Reef in Australia stretches for 1,250 miles! Some reefs grow like lacy fringes along many miles of shore. Others, called atolls, grow in a ring around large lagoons.

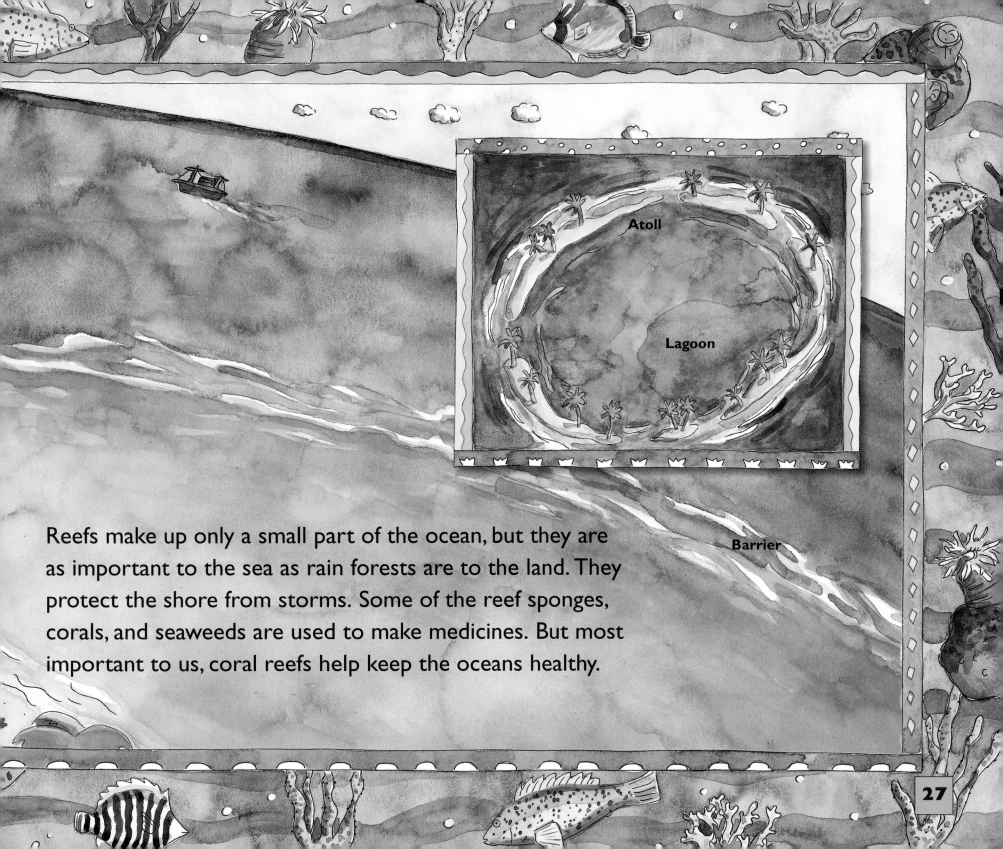

Atoll

Lagoon

Barrier

Reefs make up only a small part of the ocean, but they are as important to the sea as rain forests are to the land. They protect the shore from storms. Some of the reef sponges, corals, and seaweeds are used to make medicines. But most important to us, coral reefs help keep the oceans healthy.

For millions of years, long before people built cities, coral reefs have been living in the clear, warm waters of the world. But today, many reefs are sick. Some are dying.

To help protect coral reefs, people are trying to stop pollution from damaging them. Parks are being formed—underwater. People are studying reefs to find out what other things can be done to save them.

With knowing comes caring. With caring, people can help restore coral reefs to good health. That's good for the corals, good for the sponges, good for the fish, and good for people, too. Please come and visit a coral reef again, soon!

National Underwater Park

Filtering their food

Many of the animals living on a coral reef are attached to the sea floor. They must wait for the water to bring food to them. Some of these reef animals, like sponges, are what scientists call "filter feeders." They use their bodies to strain food from the water. Try this experiment to see how a filter feeder eats.

Here's what you'll need:

- Two large clear plastic cups
- A small, clean sponge
- Water
- Scissors
- Tablespoon
- Some lettuce, celery tops, or other leafy vegetable. You can even use blades of grass.

① Fill one cup half full of clean water. Cut some of the leaves into tiny pieces. Put 3 or 4 spoonfuls of the leaves into the glass of water. This is the "food" for your filter feeder to eat.

② Make the sponge damp. Place it over the top of the second cup. Put the cup and sponge into a sink.

③

Slowly pour the water and the plants from the first cup through the sponge. What happens to the plants as the water flows through the sponge?

④

Now look at the sponge and at the water that flowed through it.

What did you discover? (use a mirror to read)

As you poured the water through the sponge, most of the little plant parts got trapped in the holes of the sponge. The water that collected in the cup at the bottom became clean, or filtered. This is how filter-feeder animals such as sponges catch their food on a coral reef!

The artist created her art by painting with ink and gouache.

Text copyright © 2003 Sylvia A. Earle
Illustrations copyright © 2003 Bonnie Matthews

First paperback printing 2009
Paperback ISBN: 978-1-4263-0475-0

Book design by LeSales Dunworth
The text is set in Gill Sans. The display type is Sawdust Marionette.

Jump Into Science series consultant: Christine Kiel, Early Education Science Specialist

I want to thank those who have made it possible for me to spend thousands of hours
exploring coral reefs around the world and the many caring people who are trying to
protect the ocean from harm. And special thanks to David Guggenheim, Linda Glover,
Elizabeth Taylor, Gale Mead, Emma Hickerson, and Graham Grosvenor for scrutinizing
the text.—SAE

Library of Congress Cataloging-in-Publication Data available upon request.

Hardcover ISBN 0-7922-6953-5

Printed in U.S.A.
09/WOR/1

One of the world's largest nonprofit scientific and educational organizations, the National Geographic Society was founded in 1888 "for the increase and
diffusion of geographic knowledge." Fulfilling this mission, the Society educates and inspires millions every day through its magazines, books, television programs, videos,
maps and atlases, research grants, the National Geographic Bee, teacher workshops, and innovative classroom materials. The Society is supported
through membership dues, charitable gifts, and income from the sale of its educational products. This support is vital to National Geographic's mission to
increase global understanding and promote conservation of our planet through exploration, research, and education.
For more information, please call 1-800-NGS LINE (647-5463) or write to the following address:

NATIONAL GEOGRAPHIC SOCIETY
1145 17th Street N.W.
Washington, D.C. 20036-4688 U.S.A.
Visit the Society's Web site: www.nationalgeographic.com